Don't Believe
YOUR EYES!

Rob Waring, *Series Editor*

HEINLE
CENGAGE Learning™

Australia • Brazil • Japan • Korea • Mexico • Singapore • Spain • United Kingdom • United States

Words to Know

This story is set in Italy, near Genoa (dʒɛnoʊə). It happens in the small town of Camogli (kamǫlyi) in the Liguria (lɪgyʊərɪə) area.

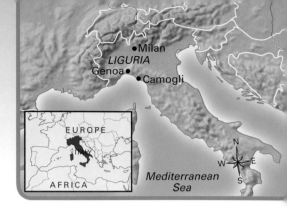

Is it real? Complete the paragraph with the words in the box.

art	coast	technique
artists	fishermen	village

Camogli is a small town, or (1)_____, in northern Italy. Camogli is on the (2)_____. It's next to the Mediterranean Sea. Many people who live in the town are (3)_____. Their job is catching fish and seafood. However, there are also several (4)_____ in the town. They create beautiful paintings and other pieces of (5)_____. They're famous for a special realistic way of painting. The (6)_____ is called *trompe l'oeil* [trɔmp lɔɪ]. Viewers often think these paintings are real things, but they're not. Look at the pictures. Which one is the photo? Which one is *trompe l'oeil*?

A Painting and a Photograph

B **Italian Homes.** Read the definitions. Label the items in the picture with the underlined words.

A balcony is a small area outside a higher-level room that one can stand or sit on.
A façade is the front of a large building.
A terrace is a flat area outside a house where you can sit.
A wall is one of the sides of a room or building.
A window is a space that has glass in it to let light and air inside.

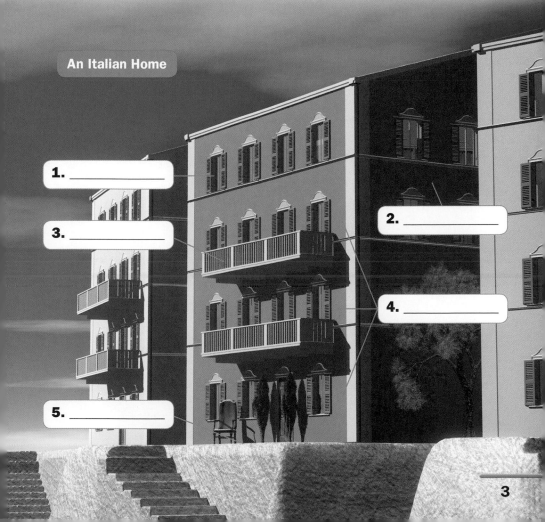

An Italian Home

1. _____

2. _____

3. _____

4. _____

5. _____

Camogli looks just like any other small town on the Italian coast. The little colored houses face the sea. The sunlight warms their beauty. But, if you look carefully at the houses and other buildings, you'll see something very interesting…and very unusual. In the town of Camogli, there are many things that seem real…but they're not.

 CD 3, Track 01

This fishing village near Genoa is full of *trompe l'oeil*—a type of art in which nothing is what it seems to be. For example, windows open—in **solid**[1] walls. There seems to be **elaborate**[2] stonework—but it isn't stonework—it's paint! And while some flowers die, other flowers live for years. Why? Because they're painted on the building!

---

[1]**solid:** hard and firm; without holes or spaces
[2]**elaborate:** detailed; made carefully from many parts

Predict

Answer the question. Then, scan page 9 to check your answers.

What are two reasons that people painted their houses with *trompe l'oeil* in the past?

Trompe l'oeil has been around for a long time. In the past, Camogli's fishermen used to paint their houses in **bright**[3] colors and unusual designs. They included things like elaborate façades and balconies on them as well. They did this so that they could see their homes easily from the water. Then, in the 1700s, this style of art became a way to make small, simple buildings look **grand**.[4] It also made them seem like they cost a lot of money.

But what about today? Well, there are still thousands of *trompe l'oeil* houses in this area of Italy. However now, there are only a few artists that are available to paint them. **Raffaella Stracca**[5] is one of these artists.

---

[3]**bright:** having a strong, light color
[4]**grand:** very large and special
[5]**Raffaella Stracca:** [rɑfaɪɛlə strɑkə]

Trompe l'oeil is in Raffaella's family. She learned this special technique, or style of painting, from her grandmother. Raffaella has not forgotten the history of *trompe l'oeil* either. She uses a mixture of old and new methods to create her work.

Raffaella says that *trompe l'oeil* is a tradition that has started to return. "You find a lot of these painted façades in the area of Liguria—a lot!" she explains. "But for a while, it seemed like no one was doing them anymore," she adds.

Becoming a good *trompe l'oeil* painter is difficult. It takes a lot of time and a lot of study. Raffaella has worked for 20 years to be able to paint stone so well that it looks real—even when you stand close to it. Like most painters, Raffaella learned *trompe l'oeil* from other artists, not in a school. However, this has become an issue these days. There are now fewer artists. Therefore, there are fewer teachers, and fewer places for new painters to learn.

It takes a lot of time to be able to paint stone that seems real.

In the city of Florence, the **Palazzo Spinelli**[6] Art School has one of the few *trompe l'oeil* programs available. There, painters study for a full year to learn how to create everything from *trompe l'oeil* stonework to **fake**[7] doors.

Most students at this school are international; they have come from other countries to learn the technique. However, they do understand that the technique is a very 'Italian' tradition. One visiting student explains, "I haven't seen anywhere else in the world [with] as much *trompe l'oeil* and **mural**[8] painting as [I've seen] here in Italy."

---

[6] **Palazzo Spinelli:** [pəlɑtsoʊ spɪnɛli]
[7] **fake:** not real
[8] **mural:** a painting that covers the wall of a building

Carlo Pere[9] is one artist who studied *trompe l'oeil* and now he's made a business out of it. His customers are often people who live in small houses or city apartments. They want to buy Pere's *trompe l'oeil* terraces and balconies to improve the appearance of their homes. Pere's *trompe l'oeil* projects can make a small apartment look much bigger.

But it's not just about appearance. Carlo feels that the purpose of *trompe l'oeil* is to bring something unexpected to a new place. He explains his feelings. "*Trompe l'oeil* means bringing the central city of Milan to the sea," he says, "or the sea to the **mountains**[10]…or even the mountains to the sea."

---

[9]**Carlo Pere:** [kɑrloʊ pɛreɪ]
[10]**mountain:** a very high hill

Carlo's painting style comes from history and the past. He uses an art book from the 1300s to study the theory of the technique. He only uses traditional-style paints and mixes them by hand.

He does all of this for one reason: to protect the *trompe l'oeil* traditions. He also believes that art should be for everyone. "It's easy to see," he says. "If we lose the *trompe l'oeil* tradition, then very little of Camogli's culture will remain. We'll have **museums**,[11] but that's not much." According to Carlo, "Culture should be seen, everyone should enjoy it."

---

[11]**museum:** a building where people can look at things related to art, history, or science

Fact Check:

1. What kind of homes do Carlo Pere's customers have?

2. What kinds of things does he paint?

3. How does Pere define *trompe l'oeil*?

4. Why does Carlo use traditional-style paints?

Fortunately, in this part of Italy, you can still see the local art and culture everywhere. It's in the streets, in the **bay**,[12] and in the **cafés**.[13] But remember, in Camogli, what you see may not be what you think it is—so don't always believe your eyes!

_____

[12] **bay:** an area of coast where the land curves in
[13] **café:** a restaurant that serves simple food and drinks

After You Read

1. On page 4, 'they're' refers to:
   A. the things in Camogli
   B. the people of Camogli
   C. the houses in Camogli
   D. the things in the sea

2. The purpose of the descriptions on page 6 is to:
   A. explain *trompe l'oeil* in detail
   B. show that some flowers can die
   C. give an example of Italian stonework
   D. show that *trompe l'oeil* is solid

3. Which is NOT a reason why *trompe l'oeil* began?
   A. Fishermen wanted to see their homes from the sea.
   B. People wanted their houses to look expensive.
   C. Designs and bright colors made homes look grand.
   D. In the 1700s, fishermen only liked bright colors.

4. In the area of Liguria, there are _____ painted façades.
   A. some
   B. many
   C. a few
   D. no

5. A good heading for page 10 is:
   A. Raffaella Learned the Techniques Quickly
   B. Fewer Teachers Equals Fewer Artists
   C. Raffaella Teaches Façade Painting
   D. Many Places to Learn Italian Art

6. Most art students believe that mural painting is:
   A. traditionally Italian
   B. not from Italy
   C. for Italians only
   D. easy to learn

7. A type of place that Carlo Pere often improves is:
   A. a big office building
   B. a house with a large terrace
   C. a home with lots of art
   D. an apartment with no balcony

8. Who are 'they' in paragraph one on page 15?
   A. artists
   B. people with terraces
   C. customers
   D. businesses

9. On page 17, the word 'reason' in paragraph two means:
   A. technique
   B. purpose
   C. situation
   D. tradition

10. What does Carlo Pere believe about culture?
    A. Everyone should see and enjoy it.
    B. Museums are the best place for it
    C. It is hard to teach everyone.
    D. Books are the best place to see it.

11. The writer probably thinks that Camogli is a:
    A. beautiful village on the coast
    B. special fishing town
    C. town with too many artists
    D. place without culture

MY NEW ART SCHOOL

Hi Everyone!

I can't believe that I'm actually here in France learning how to paint! It's really beautiful here. I've always loved art, but this is the first time I've ever taken painting lessons. There are six students in my class. We're staying in the home of a French couple in the Jura Mountains. Mr. and Mrs. Gautier are artists and they teach an art class just for us every morning. I'm learning some wonderful painting techniques. Later in the day, we visit local villages in the area. We get to spend hours enjoying the views while we paint what we see. Yesterday, I painted a beautiful village picture. I think it's quite nice!

The Jura Mountains

Painting Class

Oh, and the house we are staying in is so lovely! Mrs. Gautier's family built it in the eighteenth century. I've never seen anything like it. It looks like something in a film! It's very large and the façade has a lot of elaborate stonework. Instead of windows, all the rooms have glass doors. The best part is that each set of doors opens onto a balcony. It's just wonderful! You know me. I always sleep for a long time in the morning. But here, I get up early and sit on my balcony, just so I can watch the sun rise.

We spend a lot of our time on the private terrace in front of the house. It has become my favorite place because it's so quiet. We often eat out there and it's where we have our painting classes. Sometimes we just sit on the terrace in the evening talking and enjoying the moment. I've never had an experience quite like this, but I plan to come back again. Maybe you can join me next time. I've included a couple of pictures that I took. I hope you enjoy them.

See you soon!
Carol

CD 3, Track 02

Word Count: 308
Time: _____

Vocabulary List

art (2, 6, 9, 12, 17, 19)
artist (2, 9, 10, 15)
balcony (3, 9, 15)
bay (19)
bright (9)
café (19)
coast (2, 4)
elaborate (6, 9)
façade (3, 9, 10)
fake (12)
fishermen (2, 9)
grand (9)
mountain (15)
mural (12)
museum (17)
solid (6)
technique (2, 10, 12, 17)
terrace (3, 15)
village (2, 6)
wall (3, 6)
window (3, 6)